UNCOMFORTABLE REALITY

Uncomfortable Reality

Abuse, the Bible and the Church

A CCPAS Publication

Co-ordinated by Dr Marlene Hickin

CHURCHES' CHILD PROTECTION
ADVISORY SERVICE
Swanley

Copyright © Churches Child Protection Advisory Service 2004

First published 2004 by
Churches Child Protection Advisory Service
P.O. Box 133, Swanley, Kent BR8 7UQ.

ISBN 0 9534355 5 5

Book design and production for the publisher by
Bookprint Creative Services, P.O. Box 827, BN21 3YJ, England.
Printed in Great Britain.

CONTENTS

ACKNOWLEDGEMENTS

The writing was co-ordinated by Dr Marlene Hickin (CCPAS Council of Management Member). The group process, chaired by Andy Croall, at various times included Joan Carles, Judith Dakin, Marlene Hickin, Marion Osgood and Pauline Pearson. Consultants available to parts of the process were the Rev Geoff Maughan, the Rev Steve Chalke and Dr Yvonne Warren. The late Mark Birchall and members of the CCPAS team including Simon Bass and Bill Stone were readers. The book was edited and additions made by Julia Stacey of CCPAS.

The members of the writing group are most grateful to all of these who have assisted in the preparation of this material. We also appreciate the contributions or suggestions from Belle, Madge Bray, John and Olive Drane, Jody, Elizabeth Ogilvie, Hannah Ward, Jennifer Wild, and Gretchen G. Hull. The case studies are all true but names have been altered to preserve anonymity where requested or where considered necessary.

We are grateful for the permission we have received to use other writers' material in this book. Every effort has been made to contact copyright holders. If there are any ommissions we apologise to those concerned and we will ensure that a suitable acknowledgement is made in the next reprint.

FOREWORD

There are defining moments in life. It was the early eighties. As an independent consultant, I was chairing yet another inter-agency child protection conference for Social Services. As a senior Social Services manager, I had attended hundreds over the years. This conference had followed large-scale abuse in a church by two workers. As I was about to leave, a Social Services representative remarked, 'The trouble with these Christians is that before long the guys will be forgiven and they will be doing it again somewhere else'. I knew so often this had been so, and it horrified me, cutting me to the core. Would the church ever learn to face the damage it was doing? This chance remark birthed the Churches' Child Protection Advisory Service.

Through the years, CCPAS has listened to the stories of thousands of people affected by abuse. It has also been a pioneer in developing child protection policies, training courses and a range of other resources for churches to use. At first CCPAS worked predominantly behind the scenes but some twenty years after that decisive conference there was to be another defining moment. As we entered a new century, CCPAS decided to adopt a higher, more challenging profile.

Coincidentally (or was it?) at about the same time, a woman sat in my office telling me her story. A decade earlier her family had been torn apart by revelations of abuse. She had lost her husband, a prominent ministry, her home and her income in quick succession. Unfortunately she was misunderstood and ostracised by many of her well-meaning Christian colleagues and ten years later was still trying to pick up the pieces. Sadly we continue to hear similar stories and even more worryingly encounter scriptures being used to defend the indefensible and to excuse inaction in the face of serious crimes against children. The writer's group, which Marlene Hickin of our Council of Management agreed to co-ordinate, had its origins in this encounter.

In child protection terms there has been a significant turnround in the church over the last twenty years. Attitudes are changing and as a result a lot has happened for the good of children. But there is still a lot to be done, as this book illustrates. It is not an easy read, but then abuse is not pretty either, and it is not just about individuals. The church as an institution has also failed and needs to face up to this in order to move on. The good news, however, is that change is at the heart of the gospel. My prayer is that this book will become a defining moment in the lives of many individuals and churches.

David Pearson
Executive Director, CCPAS

Spirituality means waking up. Most people, even though they don't know it, are asleep . . . Some of us get woken up by the harsh realities of life. We suffer so much that we wake up . . . The first step to waking up is to be honest enough to admit to yourself that you don't like it. Waking up is unpleasant, you know. You are nice and comfortable . . . It's irritating to be woken up . . . If you had been in touch with reality all along you would never have been disappointed . . . Wake up. When you're ready . . .

How much are you ready to take? How much of everything you've held dear are you ready to have shattered? Wake up! . . . There has to be an attitude of openness, of willingness to discover something new . . .

de Mello

Anthony de Mello, *Awareness*, Zondervan.

INTRODUCTION

The theme of reality evolved over several months of discussion within our writing group. Our original brief from the Churches' Child Protection Advisory Service was to examine the theological aspects of the church's response to issues of abuse, paying particular attention to those whose lives have been affected by it.

We defined abuse as manipulative power used by one person over another – physically, sexually, spiritually or emotionally. Several case studies were assembled and studied in order to identify the theological themes that these had in common. Even before our first meeting had ended it had become apparent that the facing of reality, by individual Christians and by the church universally, was as huge a problem as the thorny theological issues we had discussed. In spite of all the media coverage and countless books about abuse, it became apparent there are still inherent difficulties for the church, in facing the reality of abusive behaviour in its midst.

While defining reality as 'how things really are', we acknowledge that it can be a very difficult area to tackle. An individual's perceptions and interpretation of a given situation can be extremely varied and the human capacity for self-deceit is very great. There is also undoubtedly a tendency towards self-preservation when personal security is threatened and this can consciously or unconsciously lead to self-deceit, and ultimately, deceiving other people. These behaviours are rife in both personal and public life, in the church and outside it. Facing our personal and institutional fears can be a very challenging process, even for Christians who believe that they have found the answers to the fundamental and often complex questions of life through the Bible, a church tradition or both. Somehow they can seem even more shocking in a setting in which truth and justice are said to reside, and where Jesus' exemplary life is claimed to be model and guide. It might seem unbelievable but our case studies reveal again and again that Christians and Christian leaders can ignore or minimise abusive behaviour that is clearly at odds with all that is known of the life, character and purpose of Jesus.

Initially our writing group discussed specific problems Christians might encounter in facing realities solely related to abuse. Soon, however, we found ourselves asking whether the problem was rather with facing reality in general. Do some Christians use denial and avoidance to deal with the difficult issues of faith? As the implications of the bigger picture began to impact our discussions, we wondered also if our attempts to challenge the issues of unreality in the church would bring about the change we desired. At times we felt somewhat overwhelmed and unnerved but we persevered, partly because we had uncovered questions which, in our personal lives we could not ignore, but also because we desire to see the church continuing to face and respond to the many issues surrounding abuse in a just and Christ-like way.

Over the following months, we became increasingly convinced that we needed to widen our remit, not only in the area of abuse, but also explore the ways Christians respond to how things really are.

All the case studies are based on real situations and most of them are about Christians who were at least initially, unable or unprepared to acknowledge the reality that damage had been done, let alone to make any attempt to deal with it. Some managed to, many years later.

Whilst it is true that parts of the church still lag behind in acknowledging the devastating effects of abuse, we can celebrate the fact that in many other ways, throughout history, it has stayed well ahead. Some of the most radical changes within our society have been brought about by Christians who faced reality head-on – William Wilberforce, Lord Shaftsbury, Dr Barnardo and Mother Theresa to name but a few. It makes it all the more curious that facing today's realities can be so great a problem for the church. Christians will readily admit that there are endemic problems within society but still find it almost impossible to be 'up-front' let alone 'out-front', in tackling reality within their own ranks.

We have not shied away from considering the theological aspects of facing reality but our intention in writing this material is not to produce an academic treatise. Neither is it to navel gaze. Rather, it is to show that painful real-life experiences and situations can be faced and responded to in ways which demonstrate to the world that we serve a just, upright and loving God.

So this book is written to help those wrestling with these

issues and for those with a concern for justice. We also write for leaders and others who have a particular concern about abuse within the church and we stand in support of those who work in the pastoral care field.

CHAPTER ONE

STUMBLING BLOCKS IN FACING REALITY

As stated in the introduction, a capacity for self-deceit is part of being human. Examples of our ability to function in unreality are therefore very common, even in everyday behaviour. Reactions of denial can be normal, (albeit rather embarrassing, should we ever look back on them) and in seeking possible antidotes to unreality, further questions need to be asked.

To illustrate this point the following case study exemplifies that even in seemingly trivial matters some people have a tendency towards an ostrich mentality.

CASE STUDY

'When I first had a car of my own, being the minimalist I am, I wanted to see just how far a tank of petrol would go. On the petrol gauge, when did "empty" really mean empty? I found myself developing this unreal notion that the nearer to home (and the garage round the corner) I was, the safer I was from running out. I got quite bold, and was driving past petrol stations I really should have stopped at, feeling I was actually getting further and further on "empty". I was kidding myself

I was safer and safer, completely in denial of the fact, even five minutes from home, I could run out of petrol in some crazy or possibly dangerous place and end up with both embarrassment and a long walk. This, of course, inevitably happened – the police were about to break in and move the car, it being in such a ridiculous position, just as I returned with my gallon of petrol! I learnt my lesson but I often look back in amazement at how easily we can convince ourselves of something so manifestly untrue'.

The following is more serious and shows that it is important to look at the evidence, rather than reacting at a purely emotional level that has little basis in truth.

CASE STUDY

A high-profile ministry couple met a local businessman and his wife and had a meal with them in their home. A few months later the businessman's wife was murdered and the husband was convicted and imprisoned. The ministry wife couldn't believe he had committed the crime and automatically dismissed the verdict despite evidence to the contrary. She even sent a supportive letter to the man in prison. A few months later her own husband was accused of serious sexual misconduct. This time she examined all the evidence and reluctantly accepted the allegations were true. Paradoxically, during the following years she heard various Christians comment, 'There's no way he would have done it'.

Sometimes there can be fear that our own sins, or other painful realities we desperately want to avoid, will be exposed if we hold others to account for their behaviour. That might account for the response of the woman in this scenario.

CASE STUDY

A committed Christian woman was told of an allegation of misconduct against her pastor, an allegation the pastor's wife believed to be true. The pastor and his wife had helped to disciple the woman after her conversion and she was unable to cope with the allegation against the pastor. Years later this woman acknowledged the very same problems as the pastor had, in her own family.

Lewis Smedes in his book *A Pretty Good Person*, urges us to have the courage to look at uncomfortable reality:

What makes self-deception so hard to overcome is that we never consciously set out to deceive ourselves. A liar may get up in the morning and say 'I am going to lie to my wife today.' But nobody ever says, 'I think I will lie to myself today.' This is the double treachery of self-deception: First we deceive ourselves, and then we convince ourselves that we are not deceiving ourselves . . . in a microsecond, we deny what we know and then we deny that we are denying it. . . . Why do we do it? . . . In one sense it is elementary. Reality has gone bad on us . . . reality can be so miserable that no one in his or her right mind wants to know about it . . . The way back to an honest

consciousness is the way of courage – courage to look
unwanted reality straight in the face.*

Sometimes, Christians use their faith and even the Bible to
avoid facing realities they find unpleasant, consciously or
unconsciously taking refuge behind passages which exhort
the believer to, for example, 'think about things which are
right, pure, lovely, etc.' (Philippians 4:8) in an attempt to
deny what is or has actually happened.

Dwelling on ugliness and pain is different from being
enlightened. Only when we are accurately informed about
abuse in its various guises can we be effectively equipped to
fight it and its often-devastating consequences. Hiding from
reality or glossing it over will successfully keep us out of the
battle and encourage us to live in a kind of 'virtual reality'.

Virtual reality is not a twenty-first century concept. The
truth of the matter is that Christians have been guilty of con-
structing an artificial reality; experiences, images and sounds
to embrace, a neatly packaged belief system that in time can
develop almost cultic features. The Jonestown massacre in
South America is an extreme example of this. More recently
in Waco, Texas, the world watched, horrified, when a charis-
matic leader brought about the multiple homicide of his
disillusioned followers.

CASE STUDY

A couple attended a church where the minister was very con-
trolling. church members were not allowed to visit other

*Lewis Smedes, *A Pretty Good Person*, HarperCollins.

churches. They were expected to give details of bank accounts to the leader. Before buying a car, booking a holiday or moving house, they would have to obtain his permission to do so.

Eventually they left the church and started attending another. They were amazed that they did not need to check out with the church leaders before attending a relative's funeral in another town. This church leader, by his kindness and Christ-like attitude, gave them a better understanding of the love of God and the joy that can follow when we freely submit to God's will.

Institutionalised faith and packaged belief systems are not an inevitability. The modern day Christian can more than survive in the real world, this complex and contradictory, beautiful and ugly world into which Jesus was incarnated. In this world, abuse, suffering, pain and injustice are present but so too is hope and healing, redemption and salvation. It is true, falsehoods need to be unlearned, but also truth needs to be discovered, learned, relearned and lived.

A strong grip on faith should not require a light hold on reality. However, there are strands within the church, particularly on the more extreme fringes, where faith is exhorted as though it offered a way into an alternative virtual reality, where God rules without let or hindrance and all evil and confusion are forever banished. That kind of belief is a delusion. True faith requires us to have our feet on the ground as well as our head in the clouds! Trusting in God is less about asking God to whisk us away into heaven and more about asking Him to come down to earth and help us. True faith has to be able to handle the complexities of life in a fallen world, albeit energised by a conviction that redemption is possible. Some people's experience of church is unhappy when they feel excluded due to difficult personal circumstances, such as one woman's story we came across where the pastor seemed more concerned about her regular church attendance than offering her support during her recovery from a major stroke and needed to attend therapy sessions. Thankfully there are many churches that tackle pastoral care in a positive way. We take this aspect on board in Chapter 5 of the book.

In its desire to look good the church needs to regularly check it does not react hypocritically or dishonestly when faced with unpleasant realities or is seen to be lagging behind the moral conscience of those outside the church.

CASE STUDY

There were two Christian couples. One of the couples had a mainstream evangelistic ministry and a homosexual relationship developed between the two men. The man in ministry denied impropriety and continued in his evangelistic work. Having separated from his wife, he made no attempt to remain in contact with his family who were ostracised by their original friends and left without any support. The man of the second family admitted to the sexual relationship and when condemned for his behaviour left his wife and family. They were given long-term support by the Christian community.

There is an obvious and stark contrast in the way the two families were treated. The first man denied any inappropriate behaviour and carried on in his ministry unchallenged. The other man admitted what he had done and was still condemned. His wife received substantial help but the first woman was excluded by friends and rejected by the church for 'apparently' not staying in the marriage. No one asked any questions of this man or sought to help. There were also far reaching consequences for the children involved on both sides. In this case study the church, in not facing reality or dealing with the issues appropriately, failed to respond in a way that was honest, impartial, compassionate and some would say, Christ-like. Sadly CCPAS still hears from people who are struggling to keep their faith because they, as victims of circumstance, have not received help from their church. This is not to deny the work that is being done in many churches, particularly in the area of pastoral care, which in turn is making a real difference to lives and communities.

Another reality Christians find hard to face is that of seemingly unanswered prayer.

CASE STUDY

A small girl, who was abused as a child over a prolonged period, frequently asked God, 'Please don't let him do it to me any more'. The abuse continued. Now an adult, this woman is still dealing with fear, anger and a sense of helplessness. She also finds it extremely difficult to untangle some of the inner beliefs which became a part of her because of the abuse. . . . 'This must be my fault / God is Almighty so he must have allowed it because I'm so naughty / Perhaps He's not interested: He just doesn't care'.

Christian counsellors usually agree that the 'why me, God?' question is the most difficult to answer honestly. The truth is that sometimes the question will not be answered satisfactorily. Perhaps a more honest and realistic response to this comes from the hope of redemption in any given situation coupled with God's ability to heal and restore what has been lost . . .

Why, God?

There are some things, God that I find difficult to
    understand.
I just can't make sense of all the things that happen.
Injustice, cruelty, abuse, neglect –
Why do you seem to stand on the sidelines of our
    lives?
It's just not fair – that's how I feel
And I'm angry because you didn't intervene.
Or did you?
Did you stop something from happening
That might even have been worse?
The trouble is, God, I just don't know any more.
Will the fact that I feel this way prevent you from
    loving me?
No, it can't – you're bigger than that, I know.
In fact you're so big, so powerful, that it's way beyond
    my tiny mind.

The thing is, God, that I still love you, still want you in
    control of my life.
I think that I can only wrap up these questions in my
    tears
And give them, give them up to you.

Pauline Pearson

The reason often given for our avoidance of facing how
things really are is that Christianity, the church, or even God
will be discredited if a problem becomes known. Could the
reason instead, be as author Philip Yancey suggests?

> I've noticed that Christians tend to get very angry toward
> others who sin differently than they do*.

CASE STUDY

Gemma was an outstanding young speaker, author and
Christian entrepreneur. With boundless energy and an
appealing charisma she was a pioneer in areas of great significance in the church. Many of those who rallied round her
in those early days later let her down badly, failing to
support and care for her when she died in tragic circumstances, while still in her prime. As with many attractive and
gifted Christians, the church both fêted and then rejected
her.

    Those, like Gemma who are daring and willing to challenge
the status quo can add a kind of spice to church life, create an

---

*Philip Yancey, *Soul Survivor*, Random House.

illusion of broadmindedness and might even be admired. This is so long as the challenges they issue don't put any other Christian's personal sense of safety, security or significance at risk. If any of these is threatened the response can be merciless. Unfortunately Gemma threatened all three, not from a position of strength but from a crisis of deep personal frailty. Childhood insecurity had produced in Gemma a yearning for loving acceptance, especially from men who might replace the brother and father who had been separated from her in unexpected circumstances when she was very young. Indiscriminate haste and other problems in forming relationships had brought her great heartache. However, when approaching her fortieth birthday, she had begun to acknowledge these patterns of behaviour but also her longing for a child to whom she could give the loving security she herself had lacked.

Soon afterwards, Gemma met and became engaged to a man who had freely given several hours of his time to the church but was not himself a church member. She became pregnant during the engagement but her fiancé was unable to cope with the prospect of fatherhood. The relationship ended and Gemma found herself alone, pregnant, on welfare benefits and officially disowned by most of those in her Christian leadership circle. As far as they were concerned she had stepped outside the acceptable parameters of behaviour. The reality was, however, her situation had become just too difficult a challenge for these people to deal with.

During the pregnancy Gemma was diagnosed with breast cancer. By the time the malignancy was discovered and treated it was too late to save her life. She died in near penury and in great physical and emotional pain, feeling utterly

deserted by almost all of those who had once been so supportive and had said that they loved her.

This sad and moving story is in stark contrast to the way
Jesus related to women. In John 4 we read of Jesus' meeting
with a Samaritan woman who had had five husbands and
was now living with another man. It is interesting he neither
rebuked nor disowned her even though he openly challenged her immoral lifestyle. Rather, he graciously offered
this woman something even better – 'living water', and as a
result people came 'streaming from the village to see him',
not just because of what she had told them but because they
heard him for themselves (vv 30, 42 NLT).

Christians can be theologically literate but emotionally
less so. Perhaps the emphasis on the *facts* of faith is a block to
acknowledging legitimate emotions. This does not fit Jesus'
own example of emotional health. C S Lewis wrote *The
Problem of Pain* before encountering the harsh reality of his
wife's death, which he wrote about in his book, *A Grief
Observed*. It is interesting and perhaps significant that he published the book under a pseudonym.

In spite of all the talking, preaching, writing and theological debate, there still seems to be a considerable amount
of confusion over what is right and what is wrong. If
someone has been abused by another Christian, the Christian
community (including the abused person), can find it so very
difficult to name it for what it is, a sin (and possibly a crime),
let alone respond to the situation according to Scripture and
the laws of the land which demand accountability.

CASE STUDY

As a child, Suzanne was abused by a leader at her church but she didn't see that it had affected her adversely. Years later she sought help to deal with parenting issues and depression. As she looked more deeply at her feelings, she was amazed to discover how much of what she was currently struggling with had its roots in her childhood abuse. Her relationship with God and others had been deeply eroded by the abuse of power that she had experienced. The reality for Suzanne was that childhood abuse impacted on her life as an adult. The cost has been heavy and she is still paying!

Would the earlier situation have worked out differently if Suzanne, but more seriously her church leader, had possessed a proper biblical perspective of what was right and what was wrong? One wonders what the likely outcome would have been had she told other church leaders at the time the abuse happened. Would they have been more likely to believe her or to believe their colleague?

CASE STUDY

A young woman lived in a Christian family with a rigid authoritarian father. As a child she was sexually abused by her female babysitter and as a young woman she was re-abused by her female counsellor when she sought help for the effects of the earlier abuse.

She battled with a range of responses and damage . . . her

reaction to her Dad, the process of separating her own sins as she saw them from those of her abusers, her attitude to God and to the church, her inability to trust counsellors, her mistrust of women in general and of men in leadership. Through the years she involved herself in relationships that proved unsatisfactory and that damaged her further. Thankfully she has since started to courageously address these issues and has taken great strides towards healing.

The Rev Steve Chalke in his book *The Lost Message of Jesus* considers that compartmentalising our realities is one of the most common coping strategies we adopt when we don't want to ask or face the awkward questions. Life and faith are kept separate rather than becoming intrinsically linked to the whole. Compartmentalising keeps realities and unrealities apart and it becomes easy to function by living in one compartment at a time, without reference to other parts of us. Knowledge and concerns we may have, or other beliefs we genuinely hold, are not brought into contact with each other. This lack of integration can unconsciously develop into a perceived lack of integrity. In this state we can take a decision in one area that is harmful to another including shutting down the undesirable consequences of an action or attitude, washing our hands of any responsibility in order to proceed with what we want to do or with what we consider to be the greater good. For example, my relationships with Person A and Person B impinge on each other. In order to support Person A, I might have to ignore or neglect the needs of Person B. So I rationalise the damaging effect of my action on Person B.

CASE STUDY

A minister was made aware that a member of the congregation had abused the child of a couple who regularly attended his church. His primary concern was to ensure that the abuser received pastoral support in order to stop his offending. The minister did not appreciate that the actions of this individual had caused a ripple effect within the whole congregation, starting with the child's family and then others who were friends of both parties. Most worryingly, the distressed parents of the child received no pastoral support and left the church.

One Pebble in the Pool

Only one pebble was thrown –
At least, as far as is known –
But the ripples spread wider
And wider each day.
The price became greater
That each had to pay
For the knock-on effects of sin.
Only one person abused
But others were hurt and confused
In the family and church
As the impact was felt.
The pain became greater
As more blows were dealt
And it was 'only' one person's sin.

Pauline Pearson

This is how we sometimes have to live because we are fearful or we cannot address or solve all the problems we encounter. However we need to recognise this pattern of behaviour can cause damage both to ourselves and others.

An unattractive aspect of this compartmentalising skill when considering issues of abuse is that when Christians don't want to face reality they can become very selective in their responses – e.g. posturing a 'forgive and forget' attitude towards a perpetrator to avoid having to acknowledge the seriousness of what has happened or admit to shock, disgust or sheer revulsion at what has been done. If the alleged perpetrator is a Christian or a Christian leader, it is tempting to place the allegations in one box and the good they have done in another to avoid facing both realities and then become deluded in thinking that the good must be true and the other false.

It is vital that the unthinkable is faced, that abuse happens in churches as well as in society in general. As we have already said, it is very easy to put Christians in one box and sexual offenders in another, naively believing if they are Christians they won't abuse children. The reality is that on occasions these boxes overlap, and uncomfortable as it is, some Christians do abuse children. CCPAS hears regularly from churches that have to face the reality that one of their congregation, perhaps someone who has been actively involved in the church for years, has been arrested for crimes such as downloading child pornography or abusing children in the Sunday school or youth club. If a person in a senior position in any organisation, not just the church, is accused of a serious offence (child abuse or not) there can be a tendency towards cover up, secrecy and ultimately the abuse of power. There have been several high profile cases recently involving major financial institutions and their apparent mis-appropriation of pension funds. So it can be seen the problem is not just within the church. It is particularly shocking however, when Christian organisations behave in this way. The case study recounted below show how some organisations protect themselves at any cost.

CASE STUDY

The husband of a Christian couple was in a senior Christian ministry position. His wife and adult children accused the man of a serious offence. He resigned from his employment. The circumstances were known to the employers and other colleagues, all of whom covered up the allegations. One of the employing board members thanked the wife for not causing a public scandal. He told her that this 'enabled many more people to be won to Jesus'. The man was given a big farewell party, publicised in the Christian press.

No one in the whole network made or even suggested any pastoral provision for the wife and children but interim consultancy work with another agency was found for the man. He was then promoted to a more prestigious Christian executive post. Nobody on the organisation's board made contact with his family until unsolicited approaches by third parties resulted in an official investigation. The position was subsequently withdrawn. He was then appointed by another Christian agency, which again conducted no investigation into his background or family circumstances. The man remains in this ministry role today.

It has already been mentioned that an unhealthy naivety and idealism exists amongst some Christians or Christian groups because they are unable to face the unpleasant and untidy reality of abuse. The following is an account by a minister's wife that conveys the painful consequences of such a mind-set.

CASE STUDY

Parish life as the Vicar's wife was engrossing and stimulating: opportunities for usefulness abounded. I flourished on the continuous surge of challenges, cresting each with enthusiasm. So on this particular Sunday the additional challenge of a Sunday School class could be taken in my customary stride. A quick preparatory glance at the lesson topic should be sufficient. 'Families.' Oh, that would be easy. I had very happy memories of own upbringing in a clergy family. Since I knew first hand what a good family was, it would be easy to communicate this to the girls in the class. And indeed the lesson did go very well, with plenty of illustrations from my own experience to support my enthusiastic portrayal of God's ideal for family life. As the children were leaving the classroom an attractive, vivacious girl, Wendy, stayed behind. She commented that her family was nothing like the one described. Her mother, Jody, was living with a man who was abusing Wendy sexually and who had that week threatened to throw her small brother out of the window.

As I had never encountered a case of sexual abuse I instinctively screened out that aspect of Wendy's story: it was way beyond my grasp. I now very much regret that even though I was well intentioned, I didn't face or try to help with the abuse issues in this family until much further damage had occurred. I have kept in touch with Wendy and Jody over the years, and stood alongside Wendy as she has encountered and coped with many other dramas in her life. However, by the time 'I woke up' to the devastating effects of abuse through revelations within my own family, Wendy was addicted to heroin and had two small children, each to a different father. I am happy to say that now, at long last, God's good work in her is coming to fruition within a loving Christian fellowship, which respects her and honours her gifts and qualities. It is also poignant that in having to face and deal with the abuse issues in my own family, I have found myself accepting with gratitude the solace and understanding offered by both these women.

This woman, in the early days of her ministry, sought to carry out pastoral care by fixing the problems of others. She genuinely wanted to help those in pain but she was unable to recognise and understand the reality of Jody's life because it was so different from her own cloistered upbringing in a clergy home, and she assumed that her actions were the right ones. She was also blinkered about some of her own *feelings* about situations and she was therefore sometimes blinkered about the *feelings* of others, seeking primarily to provide solutions rather than understanding.

In contrast, Jesus was completely in touch with the reality of those on the margins of society. May be this was because many of the realities Jesus confronted in his own life were so bitterly painful. It must have been a great relief to have a circle of friends who instinctively cared about him and had some understanding of his deepest 'human' feelings. His other friends, his official friends, let him down so often; many seemed incapable, even to the end, of trying to understand his pain. Jesus had been born on the margins, he had lived on the margins, made friends on the margins and died on the margins. It is easy to miss the point of Jesus' relationships with those on the fringes of society, especially his capacity for enjoying unconventional friendships. Even caring respectfully for others – those who are hungry, naked, sick, in prison, abandoned, isolated, ostracised, lonely, neglected, misunderstood, judged – doesn't often seem to come naturally to many. Christians and Christian officials can sometimes seem disinclined to form long-term personal friendships with anyone outside their own spiritual, social or economic milieu. Yet Jesus modelled the breaking of all three taboos. This inability to be personally aligned with, or on the same level as someone who has been marginalized may even come from what is taught about being a good Christian leader. Some even try to use scripture to defend their position – such as the injunction to 'come out from among them and be separate' (2 Cor 6:17).

Christian leaders can have a peculiar combination of naivety and confidence! Some instinctively respond to a situation of difficulty by addressing the *facts* in a business-like way, needing to bring closure to the new situation, instead of remaining flexible and open to changes, giving due consideration to the person's *feelings*. This may well be due to temperament rather than personal qualities or faith, but patterns for responding to reality can become set in stone without the leader realising it! Hopefully maturity brings increased awareness of the ways in which we instinctively function and of the choices we have of responding in alternative ways. This is not to deny strengths of temperament – which should always be valued – but to recognise the value in other styles also.

Some experiences, such as child abuse, are so traumatic that they are particularly difficult for the victim to face up to. But this reality is not all there is, either for the victim or for anyone else. The purpose in facing this reality is to be able to move on and leave it behind.

CHAPTER TWO

BIBLICAL, THEOLOGICAL AND SYSTEMIC ASPECTS OF FACING REALITY

Using the Bible to avoid Reality

As already suggested, the Bible can be a primary aid to avoiding reality. This strategy makes us feel not only safe, but spiritual! We can be very selective with the Bible verses, passages or stories we read and use them as a biblical security blanket. Some make us feel safe and some give comfort, which within the right context, is perfectly biblical. The problem arises when we use these scriptures simply to avoid seeing or hearing anything disturbing, keeping the blanket close at hand when personal security is under threat. Perhaps there is a tendency towards this when an individual doesn't want to face sin that impinges upon his or her own life. Maybe we spot something seriously amiss in the life of someone we like or respect. Even if we know the sin is there we certainly don't want it to be something we might have to deal with. When this happens it can be tempting to use the Bible – either directly or in some paraphrase or deduction of our own or others' making, to avoid the reality of the situation.

The following verses of scripture (some paraphrased),

when taken out of context, break the rules about doing theology responsibly.

- Love covers a multitude of sins. Prov 10:12
- In God's sight we're accounted whole, just as if we had never sinned. Acts 13:38–39
- Vengeance is mine, I will repay, says the Lord. Deut 32:35
- Whatever sins I (he, she, they) have committed are cast into the depths of the sea. Micah 7:19
- We are new creatures in Christ. 2 Cor 5:17
- God will forgive us in the same measure in which we forgive others. Luke 6:37–38
- Even if the sin is repeated so must forgiveness be repeated, to 70 times 7. Matt 18:21–22
- We are not to demand – nor to wait for – repentance or restitution: the person will answer to God for their actions, not to us. Deut 32:35
- Everyone's a sinner: who am I to cast a stone? John 8:7
- All things work together for good. Romans 8:28

Another common avoidance tool is the anxious protest, 'but God wouldn't be blessing his/her/their ministry if there were any real problem in their lives'. Using this approach, unspoken and possibly unconscious conclusions are made, that negative realities must not be true and therefore need not be faced.

It is possible to use single verses in isolation in preference to looking at the bigger picture and in so doing disregard whole swathes of Scripture. To give two examples, in 1 Samuel 13:14 God describes David as 'a man after my own heart, who will fulfil all my will' and Abraham is called 'the friend of God' (James 2:23). Whilst these descriptions are part of the whole, the biblical realities about Abraham and David include a catalogue of sins, some of them appalling. Abraham is favourably mentioned as a great hero of the faith in the New Testament but one way or another every single person associated with Abraham suffered as a consequence of his fear, greed, lack of faith, abuse, and selfishness. The Bible hides none of these unpalatable facts. The biblical accounts also detail the many painful processes God had to allow or devise to bring about change in both David and Abraham's lives.

In her book, *Equal to Serve,* Gretchen G Hull discusses this habit of majoring on some scriptures and excluding others, for instance, applauding the patriarchs, recognising God's affirmation of them, yet ignoring their weaknesses and God's consequent disappointments. It is also possible to become confused into thinking that the Bible actually condones acts of violence, rape, abuse, neglect, exploitation, theft and murder because they are written about. The Bible is true and completely trustworthy, but that does not mean everything written in it meets with God's approval.

The process of correctly interpreting scripture is an all-important one, not only for the casual reader but for preachers, teachers and evangelists alike. Most preachers and Sunday School teachers use Bible stories to illustrate particular points of importance. For instance, in the account of Abraham preparing to sacrifice Isaac as an act of obedience to God, God's reward for Abraham's faithfulness is often the main teaching point of the story. Other aspects of this passage may be read or referred to but not dealt with in any detail, if at all. Sunday School teachers and preachers should be aware that children in particular, but also adults, may form their own interpretation of the unpleasant parts of a passage leading them to an erroneous understanding of the nature of God. At times, superficially, God can *seem* to condone abusive behaviour and in some instances even initiate it. Facing and tackling this difficult reality in the right way should leave the believer with an even greater assurance of His true character. For example, in Genesis 16 we read of Hagar becoming pregnant by Abraham, despising Sarah, Abraham's wife, and then being ill-treated by her. She ran away into the desert and was met by an angel who told her to return to her mistress (i.e. Sarah) and be submissive to her. But that is not the full story! God promised Hagar many descendents, that he had heard her cry and she was to name her son Ishmael (God hears). Even after this incident we read how God made more than adequate provision for her and her son.

Within a biblical context, as in any other, abuse is defined as a manipulative usage of power by one person over another. It can be physical, emotional, sexual or spiritual. Abusive behaviour can be intended to be abusive or experienced as abusive.

At first glance, some Bible passages can give a reader the following impression:

- promotes the idea of one person having power and rights over another.
- God behaves abusively.
- God blesses men and women who behave abusively.
- God encourages abusive behaviour.
- Human beings sometimes need to curb and rebuke God for being abusive.

If someone has formed such an impression of God, they will not usually challenge the status quo. Somehow it seems wrong to question anything in the Bible that appears to permit or encourage something that is unfair or abusive. Maybe this is because many Christians are taught that to question is a slippery slope towards heresy. The result of this however can be a skewed understanding of God and a skewed understanding of what is abusive and what is not. An example of this can be found in Colossians 3:18–19. CCPAS has come across victims of domestic violence being advised by church leaders to return and be submissive to a violent partner on the basis of verse 18, ignoring the following verse that instructs husbands to love their wives and not treat them harshly.

Children are often taught in Sunday School to obey their parents (Ephesians 6:1) but much less is made of verse 4 where it says 'Don't make your children angry by the way you treat them' (NLT). Children can become very confused if their experience of being parented is abusive, whether emotional, physical, sexual or spiritual. It could also have an impact on their spiritual life and in particular how they relate to God as Father. So in order to discover what is true, false or a simply a matter of opinion about any biblical premise, it is not enough to pull together selective verses to build a sound argument. All the relevant Scripture passages should be considered, researched and honourably acknowledged, whatever the outcome . . . even if it is confusion! This might indeed be our experience as we explore biblical issues relating to abuse.

Then there is another uncomfortable reality about Scripture, one that seems to reduce even the most stalwart

amongst us to adopt ploys of avoidance. Our biblical security
blankets often come out in situations where a thorough study
of Scripture seems to throw up contrasts and apparent con-
tradictions. A good example of the complexity of some of the
issues has been demonstrated within our own period of
church history in the role of women within the church. It has,
and continues to produce a gamut of the fiercest theological
debate. Some interesting and unexpected advice on principles of tackling such topics has come from Dr. John Stott,
the President of the London Institute of Contemporary
Christianity in his book *Issues Facing Christians Today*. He
recognises the value of a new approach that he calls 'double
listening'. Where biblical text requires clarification, we might
need a different kind of double listening, allowing the Bible
to speak in its *own* different voices. We seem to find it so difficult to acknowledge that the Bible speaks in more than one
way about some important matters. This is a reality that
needs to be faced, particularly when it can occur within the
broad span of Scripture or within just one short passage.
Those of us with ears to hear about this reality – and with
plenty of inner fortitude – will find ourselves having to
engage in some challenging but enthralling double listening.

Andy Croall, in an article entitled 'Discipline or
Punishment, Parenting by Grace' (*Caring about Abuse*,
CCPAS), makes this very point:

> A quotation on discipline is taken from a scriptural misquote,
> 'spare the rod and spoil the child' . . . and is used as an
> unqualified instruction to parents to use physical punishment
> or else the child will be ill-disciplined. It is true that in Proverbs
> there are definite references to the use of a rod or staff

(Prov 23:13, 14 NIV) for discipline. However, what is too often forgotten or not even realised, is that an accurate application of their use within a biblical context is comfort and guidance (Ps 23.4)! The issue here is not whether the scriptures can be scoured to find some support for a parent striking a child or administering physical punishment, but rather whether, by considering the way our heavenly Father disciplines us, we can find some concepts to bring self discipline to the child as early as possible.

The problem is not with the Bible but with the way we sometimes want to read and apply it . . .*

Using Theology to Avoid Reality

All the material in this and the following section deal with the fundamentals of interpreting and handling scripture correctly. Although wider issues are discussed, when considering the ramifications of abuse, the same principles can and should be applied. To start with, finding one or more Bible verse on a particular topic is not 'doing theology' and we are in danger of serious error if we believe we have obtained God's stamp of approval for our unrealities by building a belief system on this basis. This is not even 'being biblical'. Being biblical is finding ALL the relevant material from scripture relating to that topic. Doing theology responsibly demands, at the very least, assembling it into a rationally organised framework and then, by drawing on the theological concepts contained in this framework, formulate a theology.

---

*John and Olive Drane, *Family Fortunes: Faith-full caring for today's families*, Darton, Longman and Todd, 2004.

The word theology means a reasoned or thought through 'word' about God. In a similar sense Jesus is described in the gospel of John as the 'Word of God' – God's accurate representation of himself. However, the way the word theology is generally used today is much broader than a study of God alone. It can be applied to any subject matter which is related to God directly or to God's dealings with mankind through history or the rest of creation. In addition, it is by no means the exclusive territory of those we might label theologians. It may come as a surprise but every Christian is a theologian in some form or other because we 'do theology' every time we apply biblical principles to our lives or the lives of others. We often avoid this important reality under the guise of an assumed humility, and by trying to absolve ourselves of any responsibility in this area by setting a few Christians apart to do our thinking for us! However, if the issues surrounding abuse within the church are to continue to be addressed, there is a need for every Christian to become accountable for their thoughts and actions in this area.

Broadening the meaning of the term theologian doesn't mean that we don't respect and take note of academic work done by the 'professionals'. The wrong we do is in according it virtual biblical status and in presenting it – in our teaching and writings – as having implicit biblical authority. We need to face the reality that once biblical material has been interpreted and organised into any body of belief by anyone, professional or not, it has of necessity become opinion mixed with truth.

Theological exploration conducted with integrity therefore requires that the biblical material accumulated is as fully representative of Scripture as possible and rationally arranged into a body of belief that does not fail to omit relevant biblical teaching. For example, the Bible verse mentioned already that 'love covers a multitude of sins' should not be used to avoid the sin of abuse or excuse the perpetrator's behaviour. Even after the effort we put into coming to the right conclusions we must still resist the impulse to give God's arbitrary seal of approval. A good example of how hard it is to do theology properly would be an attempt to devise a theology of God. The whole of scripture – all the words, concepts, stories and teaching about God needs to be taken fully into account – an almost impossible task! The more thorough our research into the gamut of biblical material, the more we find that God and God's ways are indeed past finding out. Here is an example from Romans 11:33 of how one biblical verse can actually supply a firm truth:

> Oh, the depths of the riches of wisdom and knowledge of God! How unsearchable his judgments, and his paths beyond tracing out.

The reality we need to face is that any definitive theology of God is probably doomed from the start because no amount of theological training or academic prowess can outweigh the limitations of finite human thought, understanding, exploration or expression. This is not the same as saying that God is unknowable. It is clear from scripture as a whole that, for example, God wants to be in loving relationship with humanity and that Jesus came to make this possible. Defining how this relationship works – or at least how God works in it – is where we have to be careful. God's relational behaviour in healing, guidance and miracles, all three realities being

actively borne out today, cannot be attributed to certain for-
mulae. We need to be extremely careful not to fall into the
trap of convincing ourselves of this or teaching it. For
instance, formulating a theology of prayer on Bible verses
such as 'if two of you on earth agree about anything you ask
for it will be done for you' (Matthew 18:19) and 'God will
give you the desires of your heart' (Psalm 37:4) could appear
to give a watertight doctrinal position, but such a dogmatic
and blinkered approach is not doing responsible theology. It
is imperative that everything the Bible says about prayer is
included, either in stories or explicit passages of scripture.

We also need to face the reality that any responsible
working theology, on any topic, will be influenced by our
own and others' experiences and our feelings about those
experiences. This especially needs to be recognised and
acknowledged when it comes to considering the issues surrounding abuse. Past experiences could well affect future
responses, whether we ourselves have been abused, pastored
victims, observed the church's handling of allegations,
known an alleged abuser as a friend or even been accused
ourselves. The following systematic approach should help in
doing theology responsibly whatever the area of debate:

- **Clarify the topic**: e.g. not just 'prayer' but 'answered/
  unanswered prayer'.
- **Face the reality of your current theological position**:
  you may have been studying the topic for years but
  being open and flexible will help in doing theology
  responsibly.
- **Amass all the relevant biblical material you can.** This
  includes direct words, associated words and concepts.

Do this as honourably as possible, without prejudice. At this stage do not include any material which is not actually in the Bible: if you do find ourselves adding impressions or deductions gained from your own or others' life experiences this must be identified as such.

- **Gather the viewpoints held by other Christians** and find the biblical support for their arguments.
- **Face the reality of what the study has revealed so far,** even if it's not exactly what you were hoping for.
- **Decide which of the various biblical arguments seem to have consistent biblical support** – however complex or confusing it might be to discover that there is more than one perspective.
- **Acknowledge that your theology must include a 'double listening'** to your own and others' life experiences.
- **Face the reality that these findings are the closest you have come so far** to doing responsible theology.
- **Last but by no means least** pray for the Spirit's enlightenment when reading the Scriptures. This, of course, has to be weighed with the other systemic processes in doing theology responsibly for the very reasons highlighted in this book. However, it is important here not to throw the baby out with the bath water!

Next consider which of the following factors would influence your theology in trying to decide whether or not any belief or theological position is correct:

- Everyone I respect believes it.
- It's common Christian practice.

- It's what my minister believes.
- It's what my parents taught me.
- A famous Christian leader says it.
- It's in the Prayer Book.
- I was taught it in Sunday school.
- It's written in our church ordinances and / or rules.
- It's been the Christian tradition for centuries.
- It's in a well-loved Christian hymn.
- It's in the Bible and there is no other teaching or principle in the Bible, which is in contrast or contradicts it.

In real life situations, such as allegations of abuse in our own or others lives, we might sincerely believe that in the way we react we are 'doing theology' responsibly. It is likely however that much more is happening and several strands of influence are dictating our responses. Belief, opinion, knowledge, personal feelings and genuine concerns all come into play and all interact in a complex sequence of actions and reactions. This is known as a systemic response. An example of a good systemic response to a real-life-situation is the way in which Jesus dealt with the woman caught in adultery. He presented a most interesting potpourri of biblical, theological and pastoral concepts, bringing each strand together in such a way that he was not only able to deal graciously and effectively with the woman but also take in hand the criticisms and complaints of the teachers of the law. Jesus' knowledge of Mosaic Law was second to none and the scriptures concerning adultery must therefore have been in his mind throughout the encounter. Amazingly, he didn't refer directly to them at any time in the encounter. Many Christians, however, would be quick to point out personal sin in this situation. Jesus didn't even acknowledge the religious leaders' perhaps justified concern (and professional duty?) to uphold Scripture. He could even have been considered pastorally irresponsible for not pointing out to the woman the error of her ways and the consequences of her actions.

An initial examination of Jesus' response is that he lets her off the hook to an astonishing degree. Not only is there no criticism, judgement or recrimination but his whole demeanour seems to indicate that he's gone rather soft on sin, except right at the end when in private, he tells her not to sin again. He seems to be looking beyond the immediately visible rights and wrongs of what she had done. Maybe he was more concerned about the reasons she was leading this kind of life and the noticeable absence of the man or men involved. From a purely biblical perspective Jesus, as God, had the perfect right to expose her sin. After all, he invented the commandment! But in bringing all the various strands into play he chose a very different course of action.

A Woman for God

Loved and cherished
Long before the world was shaped,
Abused, rejected
By those who should have cared,
You grew, not knowing who you were,
Not knowing your uniqueness
And specialness to God
Who made you.

Loved and cherished,
Now you are a woman grown
And yet still a child inside,
Rejected and alone.
Talented and brave,
Not knowing yet
Your specialness to God
Who made you.

Your worthiness is found
Not in what you do
But in who you are
In Him.
You have been chosen,
Picked out by God
To be the woman
He planned for you to be.

                              Pauline Pearson

In the area of abuse, the principles of forgiveness are a good
illustration of how multi-faceted, and therefore very compli-
cated, a pastoral or preaching issue can be. A whole range of
systems of belief and experience can interrelate in an intricate
web, which may then be very difficult to unravel.

CASE STUDY

A church leader has been accused of sexual abuse and a young
Christian who happened to meet him in the street re-assured
him, 'Even if you did it I still forgive you'. A friend of the victim

insisted, 'No matter what he's done you must forgive him'. Several Christians urged compassion – for the perpetrator rather than the victim – 'If he did do it I'm quite sure that he doesn't remember'. Others, including his employers and other Christians in leadership, commented, 'It's not our place to judge'. Someone on the leadership team asked whether the victim was a Christian as this was significant for him in deciding whether her word could be trusted.

Firstly, it is clear from scripture that vengeance is God's province alone but is vengeance the same as justice, and judgement the same as discernment? When these become muddled we can be ineffective in dealing with issues of abuse in a way that is just, fair and compassionate, as the case study shows. Having said this, when responding to an allegation of abuse, a cardinal rule is always to accept the victim's version when an allegation is made and ensure the allegation is passed on to the governing authorities (i.e. police or social services) responsible for conducting a full and unbiased investigation to establish the truth, particularly as there is usually a marked disparity of power, age and skills between victim and alleged perpetrator. It is not for the person receiving the allegation to pass judgement on who is more convincing, or on the basis of what has been said decide whether or not it is true.

The area of forgiveness, particularly in relation to abuse is explored in more detail later in the book, but these are two personal accounts which reflect on the process of forgiving and also of being forgiven.

FORGIVING OTHERS

For a start, forgiveness is a divine concept, as well as a divine intervention. It is not forgiveness if we put a price tag on it but our human tendency as 'forgiver' is to want full restitution and restoration. The hardest thing I've found, in endeavouring to forgive, is to realise I have to go through pain not once but twice – the pain of being hurt, and the pain of having to forgive – this seems so unfair – especially when the perpetrator can seem totally oblivious on both counts. Whatever the cost, however, forgiveness needs to be irrespective of how the forgiven feels – they may have died anyway by the time we get round to forgiving them. We need to recognise that when we forgive it benefits and blesses us, independently of any advantage or otherwise for the forgiven. Is it as painful for God to forgive, I wonder, as much as it sometimes seems for us?

BEING FORGIVEN

Each occasion on which I've been forgiven by God has been taken on its own merit, as it were – irrespective of whether or not it's happened before. I find this one of the most difficult, yet remarkable, facets of God's grace. Before I've been able to accept God's forgiveness I've had to acknowledge the consequences of forgiveness, not only the painful aspects of my own suffering! I have to regret any enjoyment I got out of it at the time and any seeming benefits. In other words I have to wish I'd never done it! Sin can be so pleasurable! I cannot bank forgiveness, entering into sin with the assurance of forgiveness tomorrow. Why not? Although we always will be forgiven, we may one day find ourselves in the position of not being able or willing to receive it. Why is it that sometimes forgiveness isn't sought? Because even the memory of the sin can be beguiling.

At the end of the day to forgive – or not to forgive – is each person's choice. Having said this, insisting on instant forgiveness, can in itself be abusive. Ann Loades writes in her chapter 'Dympna Revisited' from *The Family in Theological Perspective*:

> The process of recovery will not be fostered by misplaced injunctions to forgive and forget. To forget may be vital for survival at some stages, but the track to recovery seems to be through remembering, recalling, giving up denial, believing, digesting, feeling, sharing, letting the hurt surface, letting the hurt show in tears and anger, from all of which may come healing, and at length, perhaps, something recognisable as an appropriate model of forgiveness. Even then, in matters of the sexual abuse of children, depending on the hurt and damage, we may have to say that forgiveness has to be left to God, with the human beings involved able only to proffer some pale simulacrum of what forgiveness might mean.*

The End of the Road

Reaching this place feels like the end,
I've reached a point where there can be no turning back.
I wish I could, 'cos what I face seems so impossible.
Forgiveness? No way!

---

*Ann Loades, in Stephen Barton (ed.), *The Family in Theological Perspective*, Continuum International Publishing Group.

Why should I after all that has been done to me?
If I forgive, then it will be as though
The sins against me were unimportant and of no
    account.
If I forgive, then there'll be nothing left.
But if I don't – what then?

And God says,
'Forgiveness does not mean that
What you suffered doesn't matter any more.
It just means that my grace and my love
Can cover all that has been done to you.
As you have known forgiveness for yourself,
So you can extend the same to others.
You can, my child,
I made it possible on the bitter road
From Gethsemane to Calvary
Where forgiveness became complete'.

O God, my heart is torn
My whole body is an ocean full of tears.
Can I forgive?
God help me – not my will but yours alone.
I will step out, I will!
So, help me, God.

                              Pauline Pearson

CHAPTER THREE

PERSONAL FACTORS IN FACING REALITY

Facing reality about ourselves can be an extremely slow process. This is not necessarily because the task is unpleasant! As we've already observed, even pleasant reality – such as God's love for us – can be very hard for some of us to accept. Many facets of our personal faith have been filtered by our experiences, and this filter is partly constructed by the emotions connected to those experiences. Courage is needed to acknowledge this and to admit how very much our personal feelings and opinions have become part of our working theology. We talk freely today about computer literacy, and how important it is, but how much understanding do Christians have of emotional literacy? We don't deny that we all have emotions but how mature is our understanding of them and of how they affect us? If we hear of an allegation of abuse, for example, what are our immediate feelings? Fear? Panic? Shock? Distaste? Embarrassment? Some other feeling? And how do these feelings affect our actions?

Emotional immaturity can put biblical and other realities at risk without our even knowing it. What we feel and how our feelings affect *all we think, believe and do*, – including our biblical interpretation and theology, – is a big influence on our understanding of faith and in communicating our faith to others. Emotions are God-given and God-demonstrated, Jesus being the supreme example. Jesus not only experienced deep emotions but he exhibited them openly and unashamedly; outrage, despair, grief, cynicism, scorn, tenderness, wistfulness to name but a few. He obviously did not consider them sinful or undesirable. In spite of Jesus' example, emotions have nevertheless become a topic of much debate within Christian teaching and experience and your personal view might well be influenced by your denomination's views. Some parts of the Christian community ignore the validity of emotions whilst others undervalue or even scorn them. Some traditions even regard the display of emotion and feelings as inherently sinful. Maybe the problem here lies within certain quarters of Christian culture that accords special honour to intelligence and literacy. Having a high IQ and the various related successes (e.g. academic qualifications and book writing) is seen as extremely impressive. At the other end of the spectrum, some denominations prize the show of emotion at the expense of spiritual and intellectual maturity. But how often have we heard the assertion, particularly to new converts 'it's not feelings but facts that matter', or 'don't worry about your feelings. They're not important. No matter how we feel on any given day the facts of our faith remain secure'. Yes they do, but the security of the facts in and of themselves offer doesn't automatically mean that our grasp and understanding of them is accurate. Nor does it mean that we teach them correctly or that we help others to acknowledge appropriate feelings associated with them.

'Growing up into Christ in all things' (Ephesians 4:15,

paraphrase) probably means we need to aim for exactly that, full maturity and literacy in every part . . . spiritual, intellectual and emotional, loving God with all our heart and soul and mind and strength. How indeed can we do responsible theology on a topic – be it forgiveness, abuse or any other – without facing the fact that our study will necessitate spiritual, intellectual and emotional maturity? Even recognising this need will demand some degree of maturity on our part!

So where does emotional literacy come in? Emotional literacy and honesty are needed to inform both the process of being biblical and the process of doing theology. We need to recognise the fact that all the time we're thinking about what we read in Scripture we're also responding emotionally whether we choose to recognise this or not. Our emotions are particularly likely to influence the formation of our theology in issues about which we have strong ideas and principles. If our ideas are strong about some topic then our feelings are also probably strong. These feelings will inevitably influence how we handle biblical material and affect the weight we give to various verses or passages in our area of ministry, such as our pastoral care or preaching.

For example, the New Testament seems to state unequivocally that no adulterers – plus an amazing array of those involved in other activities – will inherit the kingdom of God. What feelings might these and similar passages induce in the reader? Whilst acknowledging the possibility that the very first hearers of the following verses could have interpreted them differently from us in the 21st century, each of them is capable of generating strong feelings such as fear, pain or anger.

- Death sentence for adulterers: Leviticus 20:10.
- Eternal separation of adulterers form God: 1 Cor 6:9.
- Jesus considers mental and physical adultery the same: Matt 5:28
- Marrying a divorced woman is adultery: Matt 5:32

Is it not easy to see why some readers would therefore take refuge in avoidance or denial? Perhaps this is exactly how theology today manages to fudge so many theological issues of great importance, unconsciously according different weight to corresponding biblical material based on personal feelings about a particular issue. Emotion is what usually kicks in first, before any biblical, theological or other reaction. How much spiritual, intellectual and emotional maturity and integrity is in reality being brought to bear therefore on what we believe and teach about many issues today? Perhaps if we were able to be more emotionally literate we would face this challenge more realistically.

One wonders, for example, what emotional processes a preacher who has recently committed adultery would have to work through, consciously or not, in order to get into the pulpit and preach about it. The degree of emotional denial involved in doing this would probably be considerable. If preachers / Sunday school teachers / pastors fail to acknowledge the influence of emotions and ploys involved in the so-called biblical processes, one wonders about the level of integrity of such ministry. If denial is the route taken then anyone can preach and teach with aplomb and conviction. If this is the reality of the situation, this must be happening all over the Christian world, including in our theological colleges and Bible schools.

As far abuse is concerned, if a Christian has a response of denial or avoidance over a trauma or dysfunction in someone else's life, this may have nothing whatever to do with theology or even personal faith, but everything to do with their level of emotional awareness. Avoiding reality can be caused by a dislike of feeling uncomfortable, but unless enough emotional maturity is present to recognise what is happening, the honesty to admit to it and the integrity to do something about it will also be lacking. Avoidance can become a kind of unspoken commitment that takes precedence over compassion, justice and courage.

Christians who respond to information about abuse in an unrealistic way might well have had a similar trauma or dysfunction in their own life. The feelings that these related experiences evoke, especially if they are as yet unrecognised and unhealed, could unconsciously determine the response. In addition any theological considerations probably won't get a look in until much later, when it might be skilfully – but again unconsciously – put to use to make the person feel right, or to look right, in the situation. Uncomfortable and perhaps frightening emotions brought up through hearing about abuse can cause an instinctive reaction that masks the person's true feelings. This can take the form of a biblical smokescreen, perhaps involving earnest discussions on theological issues such as forgiveness and not judging, or even as an extreme, about Satan wanting to destroy or to discredit Christian leaders and their ministries as well as suggesting the victims themselves have come under the influence of demonic forces. All these can make it seem as though there has been an authentic biblical response to the issue when in fact emotions are dictating a real and probably painful agenda. (Given today's statistics of women and men who have been abused it is inevitable that many Christians who hear of some allegation of abuse have themselves been abused at some previous time in their own lives.)

Returning to forgiveness, we can see again that personal factors can have a powerful influence in this area. We have already seen that issues surrounding how to do it, who is to do it, when is it to be done, whether anyone has the right to tell someone else to do it etc. can be handled in a very simplistic fashion by the church and by individual Christians, especially by those whose emotional maturity seems to be lagging behind their knowledge of Bible verses. In line with the systemic approach mentioned earlier, we can ask ourselves the following questions:

- What is our favourite Bible verse about forgiveness?
- Have we considered and do we use all the biblical material on forgiveness including Jesus' own teaching and behaviour?
- What are some of the concepts in Scripture about forgiveness even though these might not be contained or phrased in a specific verse?
- How much room for prayer with any theological application have we made, in our own lives and in the lives of others?
- What other factors (interpretation, official teaching, hymns, etc.) have informed that theology?
- What is our personal experience about being forgiven? How does this reality inform our beliefs?
- What is our experience of offering forgiveness to others? Who have we not yet forgiven? What are the feelings

associated with these experiences?

- What is our denomination's teaching on the matter? (e.g. The Absolution in the *Book of Common Prayer* states 'God pardons those who truly repent'.)
- What books have we read about forgiveness? What did they advocate? Have we incorporated this into our theology?
- How many sermons can we recall on the topic (and what effect did these have on us)?
- Which current issues about forgiveness are of concern to us personally / in our community / in the wider world, such as the destruction of the World Trade Center towers in New York, the bombs detonated in Madrid or the theatre gassing in Moscow.

After considering the above issues here are some practical questions relating to forgiveness.

- Whose role is it to forgive? (the victim, the bystander, priest, God?)
- Is there a set time-span for forgiveness? If so, who sets it?
- Is the process of forgiveness affected by the presence / absence of repentance and restitution?
- Does true forgiveness preclude seeking justice for what happened?
- Is forgetting a necessary part of forgiveness?
- Does anyone (the offender / the church / other Christians) have the right to demand that victims forgive?
- Could forgiveness actually delay repentance and healing?
- Which emotions could affect my answers?

Great damage can be done by inappropriate responses, particularly in situations of alleged abuse, which need careful and sensitive handling. A pastor or Christian friend may give their evaluation of the situation coupled with their own seemingly spiritual but emotionally illiterate response to the person involved. Although exaggerated for the purposes of the book, the following unhelpful attitudes are unfortunately not uncommon:

'Forgiveness is not optional, of course. It's not something that we have any choice about. We must forgive someone who hurts us even if they do the same thing to us again and again – in fact the Bible says that we have to keep forgiving until seventy times seven. So even if it's happened more than once that's still nothing like four hundred and ninety, is it? It's also perfectly clear in Scripture that you must forgive or God won't forgive you. I know that God will truly bless you if you do this, however hurt or angry you are.'

'I'm sure that the person is really sorry about what they have done. None of us is sinless, are we, so who are we to cast a stone at someone else? In fact you need to ask yourself what role you played in it all. Did you do anything to invite it? Did you even enjoy any of it? God has already cast their sins into the depths of the sea, just as if they had never sinned, so what right do we have to act differently?'

Trying to make someone or even pretend to forgive is foolishness. Their actions are unlikely to have an efficacious effect because the person doesn't genuinely believe in what they're doing. It could actually encourage them to be hypocritical and removing choice is not a position God ever employs. Respecting an individuals' right to choose is of paramount importance and the following is an example of good (and biblical) pastoral care.

When someone has a personal injury whether physical, emotional, sexual, or spiritual, they should be listened to and encouraged to identify and explain their thoughts and feelings, without interruption and without being told what they must or must not do. They should be reassured that the depth of their feelings are recognised and that working through these emotions might take time. An inability or unwillingness to forgive at this stage is not unusual and perfectly understandable. At the beginning they may not see forgiveness as a remote possibility but a suggestion can be made that as they work through their trauma and pain, however long that takes, they may well be shown a way through to being able to do this. They might even find that they want to forgive, as much for their own sake as for anyone else's. But there should be no time constraints on this process. They should be assured that no action will be taken to usurp their power in making their own decisions. An opportunity for prayer can be *offered* before the encounter ends. If this offer is accepted, no attempt should be made to use prayer as a preaching opportunity.

Several systemic factors have been combined in the above approach – as in Jesus' dealings with the woman caught in adultery. Theological considerations, pastoral sensitivity, spiritual awareness, biblical concerns, life experience (informing our attitude to the pain and to the person but hopefully not issuing in our giving our own opinion in any area), empathy on an emotional level, all will have contributed to the process in ministering to the person in an appropriate way.

In caring for someone who has been abused, there should not be any hasty approaches to the alleged offender(s). Where there is still a potential risk to children, such as child sexual abuse, the authorities should be informed. Jesus himself passed stern judgement on anyone harming someone defenceless, such as a child. Jesus even went so far as to say that it would be better for them to have a millstone tied round their necks and thrown into the sea! Although it would be wrong to advocate a modern-day enactment of this scenario, it is clear that Jesus felt very strongly about such issues. This can be reassuring and comforting for the person who has been harmed, particularly because victims of abuse frequently blame themselves for what has happened. Part of the manipulative behaviour of someone who abuses children and other vulnerable individuals is to make them try to share the responsibility for what has been done to them. The perpetrators of abusive behaviour often implant a sense of joint culpability or capitalise on the victim's own feelings of guilt. This can delay recovery and also delay forgiving themselves or others. So it is important to state very clearly that they are not to blame. The responsibility for the abuse is to be placed squarely on the abuser.

Sometimes, when abuse happens, there is no immediate sense of shame or degradation because there has been no physical pain. The reverse might in fact be true in that the abuser's actions generated pleasant feelings. This is not in any sense the victim's fault: in fact it increases rather than diminishes the offence of the perpetrator. One inappropriate touch can cause lifelong harm and abuse corrupts the good that God intended for human relationships. Sexual abuse frequently mars future sexual encounters but thankfully it is possible even for those affected by abuse to experience a sexual relationship that is enjoyable, enriching and part of a mature and healthy commitment.

Conflict

There's a battle going on within my soul,
For I want, Oh I want to be really whole,
To be close to God and to know him well,
But I'm angry with God – and that's hard to tell!

I wanted so much as a child to know
That he listened to me, that he loved me so,
And I called to him, 'will you help me, Lord?
Will you stop this pain?' – but he never heard.

I suppose I think, deep within my heart,
He so hated the sin that he drew apart.
For I thought that the wrong and the sins that were
  done
Were all my fault – so I cried alone.
But I want you, God, in spite of it all,
So will you listen if I dare to call?
'I'm listening, child, as I listened then.
Let's talk it through and begin again.

Pauline Pearson

CHAPTER FOUR

INSTITUTIONAL OBSTACLES IN FACING REALITY

Strange things can happen when Christians come together in an institutional formation. Group dynamics may affect the faith and integrity of some individuals, particularly when faults and frailties come to the fore. Loyalty to the group or institution sometimes takes precedence over integrity. Spiritual standards and qualities can be compromised to such an extent that the group is barely recognisable as Christian and can itself become abusive. It may also be flying the flag of Christianity but, because of its shortcomings, a watching world holds it in disdain.

Why is this and how can it happen? One factor to face, strange though it may seem, is that although the unrecognised emotions of an individual can be largely overlooked in an institutional setting they can, nevertheless, exert considerable influence within a group; in its actions, reactions and decisions in a given situation. For example, if a person in leadership has themselves been abused, shame and secrecy may now be very much a part of their life. The possibility for that person of having to deal with an abuse situation, particularly in the church, could be too terrifying even to contemplate. One of the key emotions therefore that an individual may need to confront within an institutional setting is fear. Those of us with any official position need to remind ourselves that the opposite of fear is not hate but love. Any group leadership can begin to face its fears by embracing promises from scripture, allowing these to become their bedrock of integrity and courage. For example:

> God is our refuge and strength, always ready to help in times of trouble. So we will not fear, even if earthquakes come and the mountains crumble into the sea. (Psalm 46:1–2, NLT).

'When you pass through the waters I will be with you' (Isaiah 43:2) can be an inspiration to institutions as well as to individuals. (Facing reality can at times pass us all through some very deep waters indeed.) When Jesus was crossing a lake with his disciples He said 'let us go across to the other side' not 'let us sink'! No Christian group or institution needs to fear disaster if Jesus is the focus and it is functioning with integrity. Listed here are some of the fears that seek to overwhelm church leaders, making it difficult to face and address uncomfortable realities:

- Fear of losing control of a situation.
- Fear of confrontation.
- Fear that our own assessment of a situation might be rejected or ridiculed by someone we respect.
- Fear of whom we can trust not to pass on information inappropriately (within the church or group).
- Fear of being the one to expose a situation and losing face because others don't believe us.
- Fear that the information will get into the public domain

(It is worth noting that if the situation is kept fearfully under wraps and is not confronted, then it invariably leaks out anyway. What generally makes the news are situations not handled properly by the church, e.g. cover ups).

- Fear of the power of the media.
- Fear for the general reputation of the church – and even of God?
- Fear of how it will affect other church families and individuals, especially new Christians.
- Fear of our own reactions and how we will cope.
- Fear that some of our current church projects could be jeopardised, funding withdrawn etc.
- Fear of being rejected by those we are obliged to challenge – who might be our peers or long-standing personal friends.
- Fear of offending other friends or colleagues who might disagree with our taking action, or with how we take it.
- Fear of bungling and of making the problem worse.
- Fear of change: if the situation becomes known will the church ever regain trust, confidence and stability?
- Fear of exposing ourselves to the scrutiny of state institutions (the world) and the law.
- Fear of how it reflects on leaders.

Time for Action – Sexual Abuse, The Churches and a new dawn for survivors is a report commissioned by Churches Together in Britain and Ireland and calls on churches 'to recognise the ways in which their institutional life has silenced those who have been abused and has protected those who have abused them'. Its findings are also relevant to facing reality about a

wider range of dysfunction. We include here some quotes
from the Report:

> It's hard to hear but harder to tell . . . There are some things
> people would rather not hear. It may be that the information
> being received generates emotional pain or disgust. It may be
> that hearing another person's story stirs up deeply buried
> memories in our own lives. Or it may be that, as we become
> aware of the consequences of what we are hearing, the
> enormity of it overwhelms us.*

> Where sexual abuse takes place within a church or Christian
> organizational context, fear of potential damage to the
> reputation of the church or organizations is powerful. In
> consequence there may seem to be an obligation to remain
> silent, and therefore an opportunity either for the abuse to
> continue or for others within the church or organization to fall
> prey. The numbers of those abused within a church context
> may be larger than already recognised because the survivors
> remain silent among us.*

> The 'niceness' of rural communities may lead to denial that
> anything like that can happen here or, if it does, it must be by
> an outsider. Such naivety is dangerous. People in rural
> churches often feel that because they 'know' everyone involved
> the churches are a safe place.*

Sexual Abuse, the Churches and a New Dawn for Survivors, Churches Together
in Britain and Ireland.

CASE STUDY

Some years ago David Pearson was addressing the trustees of a missionary organisation. He stressed that those who, as adults, had offended against children should not work with children again. He explained that this did not rule out repentance, forgiveness and restoration (the primary message of the gospel), but just as it would be unwise to encourage a recovering alcoholic to work in a pub, to place an offender back into a situation where they could succumb to the same temptations again was unacceptable for children and irresponsible pastorally. A trustee responded, 'Do you think then we've got it wrong?' He went on to talk about a worker who had abused a child in one country. He was brought back to the UK, counselled, and seemed genuinely repentant. He was then sent to a different country by the missionary organisation and the same thing happened again. So he was brought back for further counselling. Being again repentant, he was then placed in a third country and although the organisation had heard nothing detrimental about him since, how would the missionary organisation justify its actions in the event of further allegations of abuse against this man?

This is not an isolated incident, but thankfully CCPAS hears from far more churches and organisations today who are willing to face the kind of institutional fears already mentioned, ask for help and follow the advice outlined below.

There is a place for everyone within the church, including those who have offended. However, sexual offences are often addictive in nature, so no matter how long ago the incident(s) happened, the person who has offended may still be a risk to children and young people. Their involvement in the life of the church, therefore, should be in an area unconnected with children's and youth activities. Neither should they be allowed to undertake any leadership position within the church. Even a past offender giving out hymnbooks or taking up a collection can, in a child's, but also an adults, eyes send a subliminal message that this is someone who is incontrovertibly trustworthy.

Where someone attending a church is known to have abused children, then it is important to extend love and friendship, but the leadership will need to ensure a frank discussion takes place with the person concerned and sustain open lines communication. It will be necessary to establish clear boundaries for the protection of both children and young people but also to lessen the possibility of the adult being wrongly accused of abuse in the future. CCPAS has undertaken pioneering work in supporting and monitoring offenders in churches involving written contracts within a programme of pastoral support, and has been used by many denominations as a basis for preparing their own procedures. (See *Guidance to Churches* published by CCPAS for further information). Placing restrictions on a sexual offender is sometimes seen as a denial of God's universal forgiveness, grace and restitution, particularly when they seem repentant. Whilst it would be wrong to deny the efficacy of biblical truth, it is important to remember there is no sure and objective way to guarantee this has happened. An individual's testimony may or may not be true. It must be said again that sexual offending is often addictive and putting temptation in the way of such an individual by allowing them contact with children could lead to further offences being committed. The apostle Paul unequivocally supports this principle when he issues an instruction in 1 Corinthians 6:18 to 'flee from sexual immorality' in the best interests of the potential offender as well as the victim. Children must never be put in the path of a sex offender as a test to see if they are 'free' from their tendencies.

One indicator that an offender's repentance is genuine will be an acceptance and compliance with their contract with the church, together with the church's involvement and co-operation with external agencies who have a responsibility for monitoring the person.

Choices for the Church

There have been times when churches have tried to 'keep the lid' on situations involving immorality or abuse for fear of public exposure and recrimination. This should never be done in preference to, or at the expense of, failing to report an alleged criminal act to the police. Where there is a potential risk to children, Social Services and the Police Child Protection Team should be always be contacted. This is particularly important when dealing with sexual offences. The victim's care, health, safety and protection is paramount and should not be compromised for the sake of the reputation of any individual, Christian leader, group, project or church. It is important to remember that every individual, as a member of society, has a responsibility to fulfil certain expectations regarding the protection of children – Christians even more so.

A recent example of the problem of cover-up has been the explosion of allegations against Roman Catholic priests and

the failure of the Catholic Church to ensure that all allega-
tions/concerns are referred to Social Services or Police to be
independently investigated. The following is an extract from
an interview with Rev. Thomas Doyle OP, JCD, priest and
canon lawyer who as early as 1985 warned the Catholic hierarchy of the potential scope of the sex abuse scandal. It is
reproduced in some detail because of the prophetic insights
it contains for *all Christian institutions*:

On the wounds to the survivors of priestly sexual abuse:

[They are] profound. This is not just physical abuse that
happens to these people. The worst dimension of it, the most
painful dimension, is the spiritual abuse . . . we often hear the
term connected with the victims of 'soul rape' and 'soul
murder'. The institutional church oftentimes will respond to
questions with euphemisms: 'Well, Father inappropriately
touched this young man or young girl, and there were
boundary violations.' Those are euphemisms. That's part of the
denial. In reality, for the most part it is rape and brutalisation of
the person's body, but it's [also] their soul, and the pain and the
agony and the anguish and all that goes with that. . . . There's a
long, long way to go before the institutional church ever comes
even close to beginning the healing process.

On the bishops' sex abuse policy:

The major issue, I think, is not finding quick and efficient ways
to dispatch the accused clerics. The issue is that the bishops
have to take a long, hard, honest look at their own
responsibility, why this has been happening over the years,
why it hasn't been taken care of, and number one, why the

institutional church, through its bishops and clerics, has not responded in an honest, compassionate, caring way to the victims – why it has stiff-armed them, lied to them, stonewalled them, made them wait months if not years for responses to phone calls, treated them like the enemy, refused to believe them and, in general, consistently re-victimised them. That was going on all the way through from the time I became involved in 1985, and it's still going on.

On the Catholic leadership:

I think it requires a lot of courage and [it is] a tremendous risk to step out of the organisational mode the [bishops] are in because it's a human organisation, even though it's a church . . . there still is the cloak of organisational behaviour. One of the things that often happens with any organisation is that the leadership elite, those who are in leadership positions, begin to identify the organisation with themselves . . . there's a tremendous amount of fear that this [scandal] will impoverish or threaten the stability of the organisation, of the institution, and it already has. Severely. The damage has been done, and it will take several generations to undo that damage.

It's been difficult for the hierarchy to address this . . . this is somewhat understandable. The Catholic church is a human organisation with a political structure. Any political structure, any organization will tend to circle the wagons the more potentially embarrassing or damaging the inner problems are. The fact is, the damage has been done. Because of the stonewalls, the cover-ups, and the way they've conducted themselves, the system has caused itself tremendous damage . . . it will be rebuilt on a much different model of church leadership than what we have now.

On advice for the bishops:

I would advise them, as I've said all along, from the beginning 18 years ago: drop everything, realise that these boys and girls, men and women who were sexually abused as children, as adolescents, or as adults (and there are mostly women who are abused as adults) are not the enemy. They've been deeply, deeply, deeply hurt – devastated. They are the most important people in the church. Drop your meetings, your social events, your guest appearances. Go to them. One by one, sit in their homes, listen to them, let them cry, let them be angry, but help take some of that pain away. Do what Christ would do. Do what a real priest should do. That's all. That's very challenging. I've done it a lot with these people. I know how painful it can be and how frustrating it can be, but that's what has to be done.

Christ didn't spend his time in an office or in a church. He was out getting his hands dirty and his feet dirty with people. That's what should happen here. That's the answer, I think, ultimately . . . had the church responded, had the priests and bishops and even the laypeople responded to their true spiritual calling, to reach out to these people and not be threatened, not treat them like the enemy, but envelop them with love and compassion and care, this nightmare would have been ended.

The good news is that the evidence now indicates the Catholic church is beginning to act with courage and integrity in acknowledging their failures and in seeking to make reparation to those abused by priests and other individuals associated with it. Perhaps there are others who need to follow this example.

The next case study shows how the interests of abused children took second place to the reputation of a church. Both the church and the victims reaped the consequences of inaction. It is understandable that churches fear media attention because they are often misquoted or misunderstood. However, the church's failure to act in this situation made matters far worse, causing justifiable anger within the wider community, and of course the media had a field day.

CASE STUDY

Several years ago a regular church-goer admitted to church leaders that he had sexually abused the son of a close friend. The boy had, in fact, already told his mother, who had then relayed the details to the same church leaders. Because the church leaders feared adverse publicity for themselves as well as for the two families involved, they tried to resolve the situation behind closed doors, within the confines of the church. The man continued to abuse children over several years and his activities finally came to the attention of the public authorities through a child's confession to a teacher. The previous cover-up by the church also came to light. The church came under strong criticism for:

(i) not reporting a criminal act in the first place, many years earlier,

(ii) denying the boy and future victims any kind of justice and

(iii) allowing a sex-offender to continue abusing many more children.

False or malicious allegations are made from time to time but they are not as common as one might suppose. The much more common problem is that allegations of abuse are consistently denied. Even the person making the allegation may go back on their statement because of family pressure (or even pressure from the church). This does not mean that the abuse did not happen. Very occasionally young people make a malicious allegation because they are angry with someone; they might exaggerate an innocent touch or complain of physical assault when actually they needed restraining for their own or other people's safety. Having such accusations made against an innocent person can be devastating, but in the interests of all concerned it is still important to report *all* allegations to the police or social services. The primary aim of their investigation is to uncover the truth. If the church does not handle the matter in this way, they can justifiably be accused of cover-up. They also put the person making a false allegation in a position of power.

The most recent high profile case that demanded much media attention were the tragic circumstances surrounding the death of Victoria Climbié.

CASE STUDY

The Victoria Climbié Inquiry, whilst primarily focusing on the part played by the statutory authorities, also received evidence on the involvement of the church. This evidence indicated that Victoria was taken to three churches by her great-aunt, Marie-Therese Kouao. What followed was a catalogue of failures by these churches, despite the fact various leaders had observed unexplained injuries to Victoria's body.

When Koauo complained to one of the pastors that Victoria was incontinent, he formed the view that Victoria was possessed by an evil spirit and advised prayer and fasting. On another occasion a church worker noticed that Victoria was having difficulty walking and she wore heavy clothing covering her whole body, despite the fact it was summer and very hot. After one incident when Victoria was clearly unwell and very hungry, a church worker said in evidence that she did not seek to ensure Victoria received any medical attention because she was not aware that the child was ill.

Victoria died on 25 February 2000 and a post-mortem examination revealed 'the cause of death to be hypothermia, which had arisen in the context of malnourishment, a damp environment and restricted movement'. The examiner also found 128 separate injuries on Victoria's body, showing she had been beaten with a range of sharp and blunt instruments. No part of her body had been spared. Marks on her wrists and ankles indicated that her arms and legs had been tied together. It was the worse case of deliberate harm to a child he had ever seen.

(Quotes are from *The Victoria Climbié Inquiry, Summary and Recommendations*)

Leaders of the three churches were required to give evidence to the Inquiry chaired by Lord Laming. One newspaper article read 'A pastor at an evangelical church has told the Public Inquiry into Victoria Climbié's death that he believed the eight year old was possessed by the devil . . . in fact the child was dying in front of his eyes'. David Pearson, Executive Director of CCPAS in evidence to the Inquiry, said:

The primary failure in relation to child protection would appear to be that church leaders, having observed on Victoria obvious bruising and signs of neglect, failed to make a referral to the statutory authorities . . . the churches showed a lamentable lack of awareness of the fact that Victoria's disturbed behaviour might be indicative of abuse. A significant reason for the lack of alertness to these child protection issues may be that the church bought in, uncritically, to the notion that Victoria was demonised and it blinded them to the abuse. Although it seems Victoria herself believed that she was evil and possessed this should have been seen as a childish response to sustained emotional and psychological cruelty. By accepting, without question, this interpretation of Victoria's evidence of disturbance, the church effectively colluded with the abusers. To categorise a severely disturbed child as possessed by the devil is an extreme example of blaming the victim.

Counsel for Victoria's parents put statutory regulations for churches at the top of the list of concerns. Margot Boye told the Inquiry:

Having heard the evidence from several churches . . . if some sort of statutory regulation is not looked at there can be little doubt that some churches and religious institutions will continue to act in a manner that is totally at odds with the child's welfare.

The church leaders involved in the Inquiry had been questioned about child protection policies followed in their churches and the training they had received, but they were either inadequate or non-existent. There has definitely been a tendency towards self-righteous indignation over the shortcomings of the churches involved with Victoria, forgetting that many parts of the church are still not giving sufficient priority to child protection. CCPAS submitted results of a survey of child protection training in theological colleges to the Climbié Inquiry. The survey, carried out in early 2000, was of 99 colleges providing full-time training for at least a year. Colleges were asked what training future clergy and ministers received in child protection and about other policy and practice issues. The overall response was 70%. Responses from traditional denominational colleges was nearly 100% though not all were prepared to answer the questionnaire! There was a much poorer response from the others (43%). Over half of those responding provided no training at all. Of the remainder, the vast majority of colleges were spending between 10 and 30 minutes out of a three-year course. There were some pockets of very good practice, particularly within the traditional denominations but generally, the results of the survey make for grim reading, particularly as it was carried out some ten years after the government's *Safe from Harm* publication which emphasised the need for child protection policies and training within organisations, including churches, working with children.

The circumstances surrounding Victoria's death plainly demonstrate the need for every church to be child focused. Jesus made his position quite clear when he said 'Let the children come to me and do not hinder them, for the kingdom of God belongs to such as these' (Mark 10:14). The church is in a unique and privileged position in that, apart from schools, it has more children coming through its doors week by week than any other organisation or institution. It has a clear responsibility therefore to ensure that appropriate safe-guards are in place, particularly, as can be seen in Victoria's case, the church was her last line of defence.

Organisations may flounder when challenged by something like an allegation or suspicion of abuse. If they don't know what to do or who to turn to for help at such times, then the temptation can be to close ranks or adopt the ostrich mentality. However, this reaction makes a clear statement to any observer, 'If I can't see it, it can't hurt me. The problem isn't really there'.

When a crisis first surfaces it is very important that the church handles the situation with wisdom and sensitivity. It must be transparent in all its dealings and this may well involve consulting professional agencies such as Social Services and the police. It is sometimes suggested that where a church is involved in an allegation of abuse against a child, it should be dealt with internally. Church leaders have even tried to use scripture to justify such action. Within this context Matthew 18 is often relied upon as the guideline for dealing with allegations of abuse within the church. At the beginning of Matthew 18, we have an indication of how seriously Christ views offences against children. 'Anyone who welcomes a little child . . . in my name welcomes me, but if anyone causes one of these little ones . . . to sin, it would be better for him to have a large millstone hung around his neck and be drowned in the depths of the sea.' Verses 15–18 of this same chapter and 1 Corinthians 6:1–2, go on to deal with disputes between adults over something such as property or money, in other words a civil law suit. In such cases we read that these matters should be resolved within the body of Christ. A reading of these passages suggests a disagreement between believers that is relatively trivial. These principles are not applicable within the context of allegations of sexual abuse, or any abuse of a child. Child abuse is a criminal, not civil, matter. Indeed, if these scriptures are referring to a criminal case, then the instructions in Romans 13 about the jurisdiction of governing authorities becomes meaningless. This is the passage that refers to God's provision for dealing with criminal activity. The governing authorities are considered God's instrument for punishing wrongdoing. A case of alleged child abuse is not the same as someone taking out a civil law suit against a neighbour. It is a case of the governing authority (in this case the state) seeking the prosecution of an individual it believes has broken the laws of the land. The child effectively becomes a witness for the state because s/he was the victim of a crime. It is not an issue between two brethren, i.e. the alleged perpetrator and the minister or the alleged perpetrator and the victim, but between the child, the alleged perpetrator and the state. Reporting a crime does not go against scripture. Being a Christian does not exempt an individual from being held completely accountable for their behaviour. To put it another way, if a Christian raped, seriously assaulted, or committed some other criminal offence, any law-abiding church would not conduct an internal church investigation before, or in preference to, reporting the matter to the police. So often people do not believe that the sexual abuse of children is as serious as other offences, and yet its consequences can be more far-reaching for the individual concerned.

We know the importance of all of the following qualities but we need to continue to hold each other – and our institutions – to account in:

- showing compassion
- pursuing truth, wisdom and justice
- loving mercy
- seeking to do the will of God
- acting courageously
- making every effort to display the fruit of love, joy, peace, patience and kindness

The aim throughout is to maintain healthy relationships without covering up any abusive or criminal behaviour.

CHAPTER FIVE:

THE WAY AHEAD – MAKING A DIFFERENCE

Much of the material so far has been about bad practice and the mistakes that can be made. We can conclude from Jesus' teaching that denial and cover-up by the church grieves and dishonours God. This section offers suggestions on how we can all make a difference. As an aid to this process we have devised an action sheet at the end of the book that may help you to identify specific areas you wish to address.

- **Admit we have failed** people and God by our actions, reactions, inaction, and in closing our eyes to the possibility that Christians can and do abuse. It may have happened in our church and we did not recognise it. Maybe we did realise that abuse had happened but we dealt with it inappropriately or we covered it up in the hope that no one else would find out and give the church a bad name. Perhaps we need to acknowledge that what we felt was disgust when someone told us that they or someone they knew had been abused. We might have felt that they had brought it on themselves by what they said, or did not say, or by what they wore. We might be thinking, 'they should have said no', or 'It wouldn't have happened if they had been honouring God in their life'. Maybe we have failed to appreciate that an abuser has used cunning or sheer physical strength to get what they wanted.

- **Acknowledge to God that we have sinned** in what we have said and done (or not done). God is grieved at lack of compassion for the wounded. He is angry when sin is covered up and when abusers have continued to be allowed to hurt children or adults. (Psalm 51, and 67:64, 94)

- **Accept responsibility for our actions**. Ignorance of the law (God's and the state's) is no excuse. Siding with an abuser may have compounded the effects of the abuse. For example saying 'it couldn't be true' when an allegation was made, may have prevented the responsible course of action taking place. If we have used internal procedures to deal with the situation rather than upholding the laws of the land, we likewise have failed to accept the God-given role of the authorities to deal with crime. (Romans 13:1–5).

- **Apologise to those who have been hurt**. Have we done wrong? Say we are sorry and try to make amends. It is impossible to make things as if they had never happened but is there anything else we can do? Can we pay for counselling/therapy if requested? Although the victim might decide to seek compensation, what is really wanted so often is for those who need to apologise, to do so wholeheartedly. Also people need to be assured that things will be handled differently in the future. (Luke 19:1–10).

- **Act to change things**. We have to ensure that the way we tend the sheep, if we are in the role of the pastors, is the way Jesus himself would do, in other words with tenderness, compassion and love. We need to accept that people who have been abused will often struggle in their faith and find it hard to trust others and God. If they have been hurt by leaders, they may also resist being told what to do, even if it is legitimate and the instruction is gracious and respectful. We must be gentle and accepting of them in their pain so that they can learn that not all leaders or Christians are like the one(s) who abused them. (Isaiah chapters 58 and 61).

- **Adopt a practical approach to supporting** those affected by abuse, recognising the ramifications – victims, families, abusers, families of abusers, and the church congregation. Are you able to attend court with victims or offenders? Can you provide some extra child-care, help with household tasks, a listening ear, an understanding hug?

- **Alter the way the church operates so that** those who would seek to abuse children will find it almost impossible to do so, because of a safe church structure. Operate a child protection policy. Only use children's and youth workers who have been properly checked out and who are then adequately supported and supervised. Do not let just anyone come into the children's and youth activities. Do not allow known sex offenders to come and go as they wish but ensure that they comply with a strict code of conduct.

- **Administer correct procedures for supporting church/ mission workers.** In the past, the church, together with missionary societies and Christian agencies have not had a good track record in caring for staff and their families especially those isolated from customary networks of support. In these circumstances they can be particularly vulnerable. Procedures need to be put in place and most importantly adhered to. This includes issues such as a clear job description, a formal job application form and interviewing procedure, including references and a criminal records check, lines of accountability, support and supervision. All of these issues, together with comprehensive advice on responding appropriately to allegations of abuse are tackled in detail in the CCPAS child protection manual, *Guidance to Churches*.

A FINAL REFLECTION

Then (Jesus) returned . . . and found them asleep . . . 'Couldn't you stay awake and watch with me even one hour'? (Matt 26:40 NLT)

It was 2,000 years ago when Jesus asked this question of some of his friends. They had let him down. They had gone to sleep while he suffered alone.

From that time to today his spirit is still suffering – with groanings that cannot be uttered. How many of us, his friends, are unintentionally and soundly sleeping through his ongoing anguish over the world's great need for salvation? Of course we have no idea that we're asleep. In fact we think we're fully awake and alert. We certainly never intended to let him down. It's just that we became absorbed in all the good things we thought we were doing for him. Perhaps some of us who have been asleep, or drugged by our own success are beginning to wake up, really wanting to stay alert to watch with Jesus, whatever the cost. We intend to position ourselves closer to him, keeping him in our sights. Although we have no capacity ourselves to save the world or anyone in it, we have decided to offer him our companionship in his great ongoing task.

The more we stay awake with him the more we seem to become aware, of the depth of humanity's pain and of his pain, the more we become aware too, of his unique perspective on the great process of redemption. He is not disheartened. He is not overwhelmed. His perspective, as his pain, goes far beyond our comprehension. We might also be utterly mystified why the whole human experiment ever started in the first place. But start it did. And we're right in the thick of it, whether we like it or not. If he wants us to stay awake and watch with him it's not only our best option but it's the only thing that makes any realistic sense.

PERSONAL ACTION SHEET

Spend a few minutes considering the issue you wish to address (great or small). On a practical level consider your options for action/how you would like to respond. Find someone you trust to share and help with the challenges you face in achieving your goals.

1st ISSUE

. . . .

. . . .

My approach will be:

. . . .

. . . .

. . . .

and I will involve:

. . . .

. . . .

2ND ISSUE

. . . .

. . . .

My approach will be:

. . . .

. . . .

. . . .

and I will involve:

. . . .

. . . .

3RD ISSUE

. . . .

. . . .

My approach will be:

. . . .

. . . .

. . . .

and I will involve:

. . . .

. . . .

CCPAS is an independent Christian-based charity that provides a professional and unique service in assisting, equipping and advising churches and organisations in all areas of child protection and good working practice.

NOW AVAILABLE . . .

Churches, children and child protection

A publication detailing the results of independent research commissioned by the Churches Child Protection Advisory service into the awareness of child protection issues within churches in England. The research reflects a full spectrum of denominations, leadership, geographical location (urban/rural) and congregational size and covers issues such as training, child protection procedures, recruitment and criminal records checks.

Available for £1.50 (incl p&p) from:

The Churches Child Protection Advisory Service,
P O Box 133,
Swanley,
Kent
BR8 7UQ.

Tel: 0845 120 4550
email: info@ccpas.co.uk
Web: www.ccpas.co.uk